TRADING MADE EASY

: Easy steps and guide to a profitable day trading

By

James L.Wilson

Copyright © James L. Wilson 2022. All rights reserved.

Before this document is duplicated or reproduced in any manner, the publisher's consent must be gained. Therefore, the contents within can neither be stored electronically, transferred, nor kept in a database. Neither in Part nor full can the document be copied, scanned, faxed, or retained without approval from the publisher or creator.

Table of contents

INTRODUCTION

What is the market?

It is one spot where purchasers and client imparts.

Ordinarily, In the actual world, we say the market. On the other hand, we express this as a commercial center.

It is only a foundation of correspondence among purchasers and dealers.

In the market, both actual items and administrations are sold.

The market is an establishment where at least 2 specialists trade something.

An establishment can be an actual spot or a theoretical spot. It can likewise be difficult to characterize and draw limits where one market begins and the other finishes.

Where does the cash come from

For the most part, there exists a thing or things that others want, similar to gold. Individuals might stamp the gold to show the amount it gauges, yet it's as yet gold and exchanged like some other pieces of gold and the stamp is essentially a way to indicate to others the amount of gold that thing possesses. This is known as product cash. Legislatures might guarantee these stepped pieces as a norm, however, you don't mind since it's gold and you realize others need gold.

Presently, you have an excessive amount of gold to simply haul around so you choose to give it to somebody to keep. Consequently, he gives you a receipt that says "This receipt allows you later to guarantee the 1 lb of gold you gave me". Others understand what this receipt does, so they choose to exchange receipts instead of haul around coins. In the end, somebody truly strong, similar to the public authority, will need to control these receipts. This is known as agent cash.

Ultimately, legislatures normalize these notes into money. At the point when they get too enormous or conclude they need more command over what this money is worth, they in the end break from it and express something like "Your receipts aren't great for gold anymore, yet you can involve them for charges". Since everybody needs to cover charges, individuals are for the most part glad to keep utilizing your money. This is known as government-issued currency.

Who Creates Money?

Changes in the amount of cash might start with activities of the Federal Reserve System (the national bank) [a private banking cartel], store foundations (basically business banks), or the public [that would be you!]. The significant control, in any case, rests with the national bank [Private Bankers].

The genuine course of cash creation happens basically in banks. As noted before, checkable liabilities [Promissory Notes] of banks are cash. These liabilities [something owed] are clients' records. They increment when clients store cash [federal hold notes otherwise known as outsider promissory notes] and take a look at [Bills of

Exchange] and when the returns of credits made by [your promissory note] the banks are credited to borrower's records. Without any lawful save necessities, banks can develop stores by expanding advances [more promissory notes] and ventures insofar as they keep sufficient cash [third party promissory notes] close by to recover anything sums the holders of stores need to change over into money. This one-of-a-kind quality of the financial business was found a long while back.

Do you see a specific theme to this? Could the Banks don't loan you anything? The advance is made by the promissory note. They are purchasing your promissory note to give you a credit! Their acquisition of your promissory note makes a responsibility on their books.

Cash is an obligation. All cash is made by banks and is in some structure owed back to banks, with a premium.

Both national banks and ordinary banks reserve the option to make cash. In many purviews no other person does. Quite, the public authority has in all likelihood offered the option to make cash to the national bank, and will itself need to get cash from it.

National banks can make cash voluntarily and unbounded, however, they must keep the economy stable, so they follow specific standards. They could trade government securities to manage the all-out supply of cash available for use and to keep away from expansion or collapse. They could likewise make direct credits, generally to ordinary banks. They fluctuate the financing cost of such credits (the great rate) to impact the economy, to animate, or put acquiring sometime later down.

Customary banks have specific limitations on how much cash they can make. For the most part, there's a save proportion that determines how much cash they can make comparisons to the stores they hold, including cash they've acquired from the national bank. Note that they don't for any reason loan out the contributors' cash. The cash they make is designated "credits", however, there's entirely being advanced out. The credit is fundamentally a few numbers added to the record of the "borrower", which he can then proceed to spend. Yet, he wants to bring them back sooner or later, and concoct the interest.

Note that the cash made in one bank is probably going to be kept in different banks en route, as it gets spent or contributed, which again figures in with the stores of those banks, permitting them to make more cash (issue more credits).

That makes a numerical movement which intends that, if we utilize the U.S. for instance, in total around 10 fold the amount of can is loaned out than what is saved.

At the point when advances are taken care of by banks, the chief is annihilated. For example, the cash that was made in any case is then annihilated.

Note that cash isn't made or dispensed in light of the amount anyone needs or merits. Cash is made and dispensed by banks solely founded on how well a borrower can exhibit that he will want to duplicate it and pay it back with revenue. For example, cash itself is made for the benefit, of a business.

That is by and large somewhat confidential. Most financial specialists will leave out the center of it, the making of credit out of nowhere and the benefitting from the interest on it, and will just own up to it "in private", if by any means.

How does the market function

A securities exchange works the same as an Auction market, So the cost of stocks chose by the financial backers themselves.

Like DII, FII, Retail, Gov, and so forth.

Supply request is a straightforward rationale on which financial exchange works.

Assuming Most financial backers think that organization has great long-haul potential to develop stock will go high.

Stocks additionally give transient moves in light of information, those generally on account of dealers.

When news affirms realities genuine development begins.

For the time being, a market is a democratic machine. Yet, in the long haul, the market is a weighing machine.

Section 1: How the securities exchange works

Section 2: How can one assess Stocks Basics of a Stock Market

History: quite sometime in the past, people ran organizations with simply their cash. The organizations they ran were little and they developed the organizations just for their benefit. Nonetheless, not all organizations can be worked with your cash. Imagine a scenario in which you needed to fabricate another plant that costs more than 1,000,000 bucks. Banks will not loan cash to youthful organizations and your companions will not have that much.

In the fifteenth sixteenth 100 years as the Europeans began investigating Asia and the Americas, the huge pioneers felt they required a truckload of cash and their lords were not giving them any longer. The rich folks requested a ton of interest. In this manner, they believed they need to fundraise from a lot of ordinary citizens. Consequently, in 1602, the Dutch East Indian organization turned into the primary organization to give portions of its organization in the Amsterdam Stock Exchange and get exchanged consistently.

What is a Stock?

Stocks in an organization give you a portion of the organization's future benefits as a trade-off for the capital contributed. For example, assuming you purchase 1 supply of Apple now, you will be guaranteed one-billionth of Apple's benefits from here on out (as there are very nearly a billion such stocks that Apple has given at this point).

Posting: In a financial exchange, 1000s of organizations are recorded and these organizations (called public organizations - as they have given out their portions to the normal public) pay a charge to the trades, alongside a guarantee to give exceedingly significant data to the business sectors. Consequently, they get a chance to place their organization on the securities exchange's board and can get cash from individuals visiting the market. Whenever an organization's first stock shows up on the financial exchange's board is called an IPO (Initial Public Offer).

Merchants:

Conceptually, a stock trade is like eBay. These folks permit organizations to be recorded and associate with the purchasers and vendors. Since a huge number of individuals exchange the market and it is basically outside the realm of possibilities for these trades to think about every one of the people, they have relegated specialists who act between the trades and the people.

How can one value a stock Basic Terminology:

We will utilize the term EPS (Earnings per share) which is precisely as it sounds. It is the benefits of the organization partitioned by several offers. For example, Apple has $41 billion in benefits and around 950 million offers, giving an EPS of around 41000/950 = $44/share. Consequently, if you own a portion of Apple, you are qualified for 44 bucks of Apple's benefits this year.

Working out Share cost:

To assess the amount you want to pay for that 1 Apple stock you want to do a basic expansion of all the income you will get

Stock Price = EPS in Year 1 + EPS in Year 2 +...

Presently, you realize that a dollar procured a long time from now isn't equivalent to a dollar acquired at this point. Since there is a financing cost included and the cash you get in 10 years is less commendable than the cash you have now. Subsequently, you want to change that formulae.

Principal benefits of a stock exchange:

1. Beginning/fabricating a business: The market allows organizations to get cash from an enormous number of individuals. That implies there are more choices to get cash to construct a business.

2. Spreading risk: It gives you to spread the risk of business access to an enormous number of individuals. Since every individual is effective in financial planning just a little piece of their pay in a load of a specific organization, the chance of a

solitary organization falling doesn't essentially influence financial backers.

3. Aggregate assessment of significant worth.

Synopsis: Modern companies require a ton of capital, which is past the span of a couple of people. Markets assist organizations with fund-raising from countless individuals and together these financial backers esteem their organization. The hypothesis is that when an enormous number of individuals do their free valuation, the organization's cost draws all the nearer to its optimal worth.

Stock Exchange phycology.

"For the time being, the market is a fluctuating machine. Yet, in the long haul, the market is a weighing machine.

What are a few severe insights about day exchanging that beginners ought to be aware of?

Day exchanging looks misleading and straightforward yet genuinely more than 90% of the individuals who enter the market lose all their cash. Why?

It's straightforward to assume you watch a round of tennis and conclude this is fun and simple and needs to play. Don't sweat it, as a fledgling you'll play and learn with players at your level. Provided that and when you become great say long term down the line-will you get the honor to play with a truly predominant player not to mention an ace?

Presently balance this with day exchanging. In the very beginning, damnation your most memorable moment, you'll be facing the geniuses. Indeed you'll get your portion of amateurs' karma yet that will just make you put significantly more in your record. Then, at that point, when you lose you'll lose hugely.

What's the solution?

You can't figure out how to exchange by being uninvolved or even paper exchanging (it's simply not equivalent to there's no ravenousness or dread - the two of which you want to figure out how to battle). So begin little, tiny.

Center around first gaining the nuts and bolts from great specialized investigation books, recordings, and so on. This cycle will be deeply rooted as learning in exchanging never stops however I'd say give it somewhere around a half year to long term. During this time you can exchange tiny.

If following a half year you have 90% of your underlying capital praise yourself. You have the discipline to begin gradually going greater. Yet, gradual steps.

Continuously have hard stop losses, it's a non-debatable never normal down or add cash to a horrible exchange.

Keep your benefit targets little, don't be avaricious, predictable little benefits will add up. Try not to envision you'll twofold your cash or begin making lacs each month. It's intense as you're battling the professionals for your portion of beginner cash.

The cash-in-day exchanging goes from the washouts to the champs of the day. Cash isn't put there by stock representatives or the "market". This implies solidified professionals are getting by taking out the suckers. Recollect that.

Adhere to your arrangement, have hard stops, and log out whenever you've created your gain target or most extreme permitted misfortune for the afternoon. Do this process again.

Stock exchanging isn't excessively complicated, it's not difficult to realize however what's significant is to stay away from huge misfortunes and terrible days.

A great many people bust a very long time of benefits while possibly not the majority of their records on only a couple of exchanges or a terrible run. If it isn't resolving go home for the week. On the off chance that it isn't working requires longer investment off.

The economic situations that you prevail in are recurrent, so assuming you're patient they'll return. Likewise, with time you'll figure out how to exchange all economic situations yet provided that you have cash in the record and aren't scarred by your misfortunes. Recollect the people who are still in the market after say 5 years of this day-to-day fight will take cash from the new part of suckers who come in with each buyer market. Brutal however evident.

Basically day exchanging conveys a high risk. There will never be an assurance that you will bring in cash. As indicated by the U.S. Protections and Exchange Commission, "informal investors ordinarily experience extreme monetary misfortunes in their initial, not many long stretches of exchanging." Day exchanging is costly.

Exceptionally Risky: One of the essential weaknesses of intraday exchanging is that it is profoundly hazardous, which is the motivation behind why most dealers lose their underlying capital within 2-3 months of beginning this work. Chance and exchange the board is the way to progress in intraday exchanging and one should figure out how to carefully consolidate them.

Not a temporary work: Intraday exchanging requires an individual to sit before his/her work area from 9:00 AM - 3:30 PM, track the business sectors proficiently, and afterward have a speculative inclination. It demands full-time responsibility, accuracy, and a ton of discipline which is simply unrealistic with temporary work.

Needs intense concentration, meticulousness, and mental Strength: Some merchants execute exchanges like clockwork on Intraday. In that situation, floating off to another work, or taking a gander at the cell phone can make us miss an exchange. An individual's regard for little subtleties and concentration should be exceptionally high over the day in intraday exchanging Intraday is intellectually debilitating and isn't a great fit for everybody.

Unpredictability: The instability of a 5-minute or a 30-minute outline is exceptionally high when contrasted with a month-to-month or a 6-month graph. To this end, it is somewhat more straightforward to exchange the drawn-out diagrams.

You, Will, Lose More Than You Earn at First: Day exchanging is here and there alluded to as a make easy money trick, and for individuals who are enticed by certain applications or clubs, this is valid. You'll set down hundreds

or on the other hand a large number of dollars to an outsider with expectations of awakening a mogul just to be in devastating obligation. The more you bet, the more you need to lose, and the stakes can be incredibly high for somebody putting their whole reserve funds on the table.

Exchanging Illiquid Stocks: Trading in illiquid stocks is the normal and quite possibly of the greatest mix-up informal investors make, which is because of the absence of examination. They should comprehend that the liquidity of stock assumes a crucial part in intraday exchanging.

We should comprehend with a model given underneath:

Envision what is going on where a merchant is purchasing a particular stock in the early morning and wanting to sell it before the market closes at a benefit yet winds up having no purchasers prepared for the stock bought. This could prompt a broker's sell request not to get executed and the stock being conveyed to you in their Demat account. In this manner, it's dependably essential to put the exchange organizations with a ton of liquidity in their pieces of the pie.

Not Taking a 360 Degree View of the Market: Many intraday dealers get the pattern and ride till the finish of the end day, yet it's not basic as that. As key financial backers, they need to go inside and out and examine the stock presentation and the intraday dealer necessities to get into the subtleties of the exchange structure. As intraday brokers, they should comprehend the pattern running on the lookout and take a 360-degree perspective available to all the more likely to figure out the market.

Fostering a Negative Attitude or Being excessively close to home: The essential rule of intraday exchanging isn't to get excessively joined to the benefit and misfortunes and get discouraged in the event of losing cash while performing intraday exchanging. A merchant should continuously keep their feelings to the side and shouldn't allow misfortunes to come in their manner, and halting exchanging by and large will diminish their possibilities of setbacks. In any case, it will foster a negative demeanor towards the securities exchanges. They should constantly comparatively treat benefit and misfortune and spotlight advancement by observing the guidelines to learn while doing intraday exchanging.

Disregarding the Trading Plan and the Trading Diary: The exchanging plan and the exchanging journal are the fundamental things that intraday dealers overlook. How about we take a gander at the exchange plan first?

The exchanging plan snatches and frameworks how intraday exchanges should be considered and executed. This comprises benefit targets, stop misfortune, elements to consider, and choosing the right exchanging hours. An exchanging plan is a whole book for the exchanging action that a broker requires to stick rigorously to. Then again, the exchanging journal records every one of the brokers that occurred during the single exchanging day and the legitimization and the EOD examination of execution.

The exchanging journal assists the dealer with tracking down feeble regions and further developing their exchanging system holes. On the off chance that a merchant doesn't give significance to the exchanging plan and the exchanging journal, making progress as an intraday dealer will be troublesome.

What is the essential rule of intraday exchanging?

The essential rule of intraday exchanging isn't to get excessively connected to the benefit and misfortunes and get discouraged in the event of losing cash while performing intraday exchanging.

What is a stop-loss request?

The stop-misfortune request is a kind of request where the dealer teaches the representative to sell the stock straightaway when the market falls under a foreordained cost during the exchanging day.

What are exchanging plans?

The exchanging plan gets and frames how intraday exchanges should be considered and executed. This comprises of benefit targets, stop misfortune, elements to consider, and choosing the right exchanging hours

Stock Exchange phycology

You will discover that brain science is a critical part of being a fruitful merchant. Exchanging is a psyche game. You should dominate your considerations and your feelings. The second you let it outwit you is the second you become the cause of all your problems.

Exchanging is trying all things considered so you can't stand to impede in your particular manner. Ace your brain research, and make an exceptional life.

Exchanging brain research addresses different parts of an individual's character and conduct that impact their exchanging rehearses. The brain science of exchanging can be all around as significant as different factors like information, experience, and expertise in deciding to exchange achievement.

It takes a great deal of expertise to exchange the monetary business sectors effectively. It consolidates the organization's fundamental trying abilities with deciding the bearing of the stock pattern. In any case, these specialized abilities are not generally as significant as the broker's idea.

Our most noteworthy adversary, when we exchange, is inside you. Achievement will possibly come assuming that you figure out how to get a grip on your feelings. Edwin Lefevre's book Reminiscences of

Alert

Energy (and apprehension about losing the open door) frequently allure us to enter the market before it is protected to do as such. After a drop in the number of circles, most may bomb before one can pass. Likewise, the profound effect of a beneficial business might make us neglect to focus on the way that this pattern is on the decay.

Tolerance

Hang tight for proper economic situations before exchanging. There are times when it is shrewd to leave the market and turn away.

Certainty

Be striking in your convictions: Take moves toward safeguarding your benefit when you see that the pattern is debilitating, yet remain solid and don't let the apprehension about losing some portion of your benefit lessen your judgment. Odds are good that the training will continue its vertical pattern.

Separation
Center around innovation as opposed to cash. Assuming that your exchange is precise, benefits will follow.

Remain sincerely associated with the market. Abstain from becoming involved with the transient delights of life. Screen seeing is an indication of discussion: assuming that you continually check costs or gaze at diagrams for quite a long time it is an indication that you don't know of your procedure and you might miss out.

Center

Center around long-haul outlines and don't attempt to get each second. The most productive exchange is in getting enormous patterns.

Look for something incredible

Contributing includes understanding the potential outcomes - not the assurances. Nobody can continuously foresee the market precisely. Keep away from the attitude of card sharks.

Normal up - not down

Assuming you increment your position when the cost is against you, you are liable for covering your misfortunes. When the value begins to move to proceed that way is probable. All things considered, increment your openness when the market ends up being correct and pertinent.

Limit your misfortunes

Use stop misfortune to safeguard your funds. At the point when the suspension misfortune begins, accomplish something rapidly - don't hold back.

The greatest misstep you can make is to clutch a falling cell, trusting you will recuperate. Falling stocks tend to miss the mark regarding what you anticipated that they should do. Ultimately, you are compelled to sell, squandering your cash.

The human instinct for what it's worth, numerous dealers and financial backers disregard these principles when they initially start. It very well may be a costly illustration.

Control your feelings and try not to clear the group. Go with predictable choices because of sound specialized examination.

Exchanging is about mental execution for what it's worth about fostering areas of strength for a. Without the intellectual ability to adhere to the framework, the best system on the planet will sit

28

idle. Best books on exchanging brain research further develop our exchanging technique. Great brokers change and carry out a methodology as well as perceive their qualities (like discipline and tolerance) and foster them, which
permits them to be more powerful in executing their strategies. An assortment of books can assist dealers with doing whatever it may take to comprehend how brain research functions in money management.

What to exchange?

This implies which resource is the most unpredictable, given the ongoing influence of necessities accessible to a retail financial backer. All things considered, this is the request that I would rank the monetary instruments in, given their standard unpredictability (for example their cost return swings) as well as the influence that a representative would sensibly permit:

Forex/Index Options: If value choices are like betting (see underneath), then prospects' choices resemble betting on steroids. Prospects, as a resource class itself, is as of now exceptionally turned in any case. Most merchants will work out your prospect's choices edge necessities in light of the SPAN margining framework, and that implies you will not need to provide as much cash on each exchange as you would on value choices. Entire fortunes can be made or lost in a solitary day, while possibly not prior.

Value Options (likewise called investment opportunities): It's difficult to give a decent natural clarification for what choices are, yet you can consider them side-wagers on stocks that can likewise be utilized as a kind of protection (assuming you own a stock and purchase a side-bet on them falling, okay, you've supported your venture). This monetary instrument is very like a fate choice, however, merchants will expect you to provide all the cash you would lose in a more awful case situation. Except if you're in the choices market for portfolio assurance or you're sufficiently modern to sell them for money (à la iron condors or butterflies), you're presumably betting. Once more, entire fortunes can be made or lost in a solitary day, while possibly not prior.

Foreign Exchange (Forex): Yes, this is monetary forms - Euros, dollars, yens. You might feel like monetary forms scarcely move - like Europe used to be costly it's as yet costly. But since monetary forms scarcely move, the law permits representatives to present you with 50x influence. Indeed, 50x influence!! Indeed, even the poor among us had some control over more than $1 million of notional worth at those levels. You can win enormous or lose hugely. Over ongoing years, be that as it may, most forex agents have gotten control over how much influence they provide for retail financial backers, particularly after certain merchants kicked the bucket

Futuress: Futures were designed to assist ranchers with overseeing the selling of their harvests. Practically speaking, most examiners exchanging prospects have no aim of taking conveyance on the corn, pork tummies, or barrel of oil. Indeed, even bitcoin has a fates contract now. The thing with fates is that your agent doesn't anticipate that you should put all the cash down that the whole prospect's contract is worth. For instance, every gold prospects contract is for the buy or offer of 100 troy oz. of fine gold, which at the ongoing cost of $1,743 implies that every prospects contract is valued at $174,300. Yet, you could purchase a gold prospects agreement and control $174,300 of gold by just putting down $10,065 (the underlying fates edge). That is over 17x the influence!

Utilized ETFs: Leveraged ETFs are worked to reproduce returns that can be 2-3x that of the general financial exchange as well as another resource. You ought to know that because of the standard of science, these monetary instruments in all actuality do lose esteem over the long haul (for not a great explanation other than how they're made). So on the off chance that oil made a 10% return this year, the 2x utilized oil ETF will return fundamentally under 20%. Google "utilized ETF exchange" on the off chance that you're keen on a careful clarification.

Cryptocurrency: I've positioned them here accepting for the time being that you're exchanging them with next to no use. Bitcoin can likewise be exchanged as a prospects agreement, and some digital currency trades offer influence (some even up to forex levels), so crypto is truly YMMV in light of the influence you use.

Stocks: Regulation T in the U.S. permits merchants to surrender retail financial backers to 2x influence (or 4x influence under unique Day Trading guidelines) through edge exchanging.

High return Bonds: High yield securities (additionally called garbage securities) will as a rule move significantly more like stocks than venture grade securities. Thusly, you will for the most part see high return bonds provided in cost estimates as opposed to in acknowledged spreads (similarly with venture grade bonds).

Venture Grade Bonds: Investment-grade securities are given by profoundly appraised, normally enormous enterprises that can almost certainly take care of their obligation. Their costs scarcely move. Thusly, they are generally cited as far as spreads over Treasury bonds.

You shouldn't simply begin placing cash into whatever is at the first spot on this list. The monetary instruments that can be generally productive to exchange are additionally the ones where you can lose all your cash the speediest.

Tools used in stock exchanging

At the point when I dealt with an exchanging work area at a mutual fund, we utilized Bloomberg and different exchanging stages (Smart connect, TradeWeb, BrokerTec, Worldwatch) vigorously. Bloomberg falls into the 'should have' classification for most merchants, however, there are options... Exchanging stages are intended for the kind of exchanging you are doing. For our purposes, they were for execution, however for cost disclosure also. All the other things we wanted were especially worked by us in succeed or C#. We did no mechanized execution, so these devices were only for our bookkeeping, risk the executives, examination, and so on. It is very normal for brokers to have little custom exercise manuals with VBA or programs worked for them by their group or a quant/programming office. Such things can fall into any classification. The ones we invested huge energy fabricating and keeping up with were all unquestionable requirements.

1. **System of rewards.** I'm certain that few out of every odd individual can set aside a huge installment immediately and hence the primary store extra aides him. Here it is 35%. The most fascinating element here is the chance to get a reward on the subsequent store and the following ones. 20-25%. you have additional cash. Isn't just perfect. The circumstances for pulling out this cash are not confounded!
2. **Leverage 1:** 2000. This likewise applies to the subject of a little store. I think you comprehend. On the off chance that you utilize such an influence, your chances promptly increment, however, remember that this is likewise a risk. Open AAFX Trading Demo Account and take a stab at exchanging. You want an exchange procedure.

3.**Trading stage Metatrader 5**. This is a magnificent exchanging programming for astounding specialized examinations. There is a large number of markers here. What's more, there is a request book, and that implies that you get the most

4. We likewise had utilization of the company's administrative center framework for exchange goals, bookkeeping, risk the board, and so on. Having such a system is certainly prudent. We utilized it to check against our bookkeeping success. Ultimately they set up their framework to create day-to-day risks the board reports. Additionally prudent.

5. There are a lot of exchanging instruments that are ideal to have, however, we generally rested easier thinking about utilizing our own devices that we made because we needed total straightforwardness and control. So I would put many outsider examination apparatuses in here.

We exchanged generally US Treasury bonds and prospects, so my experience might vary from most.

I would agree that it's vital to utilize devices that are notable in the dealer's local area. All things considered, with regards to financial planning it's smarter to be protected than sorry.

Fundamentally, there are many devices to browse today however I might want to zero in on those which have been assisting me with exchanging for some time now. I discuss Streetbeat and its pre-planned systems and signs. What I like most about it is the wellsprings of data it utilizations to make signals. It's not just considered normal and public information which is utilized by many exchanging devices today. It's even data, say, about the quantity of web-based feature supporters. For example, if it's more than it was normal, it's a sign to put resources into. I make it more straightforward than it is nevertheless it's only for better comprehension. Furthermore, I find it a very valuable and lovely speculation diminishing.

In this cutting-edge computerized time, Investors and sellers are involving exchanging programming for exchanging. This product is likewise utilized for the investigation of items including stocks, prospects, monetary standards, and choices. The specialized investigation program contains a few modules for controlling request positions and sorting out proficient business growth strategies. For performing specialized investigation, there are extra decisions available, including conversation rooms, selective apparatuses, information outlines, and pointers.

Exchanging and contributing experts currently have a superior comprehension of the nuances of directing exchanges and contributing thanks to specialized investigation devices. Then there are modules for automatic and paper exchanging that are additionally available. Alongside this, paper exchanging gives sans risk exchange components without implying genuine cash, automatic exchanging guarantees the computerization of exchange-related exercises. A few fundamental elements of specialized examination programming for intraday exchanging are empowered when it is in activity, helping brokers and financial backers in settling on smart speculation choices.

What are the elements of stock exchanging tools.

A full help diagramming program. Indeed, every intermediary has a stripped-down outlining programming program however you will require a further developed graphing program that gives the accompanying instruments inside the diagramming programming.

The capacity to set YOUR boundaries and settings for your exchanging style. Each exchanging style calls for various period settings, various markers, and different sign examples for passage and ways out.

Examines, Sorts, Screeners. These are a basic arrangement of directions you can make inside the product. Normally a full help outlining system will permit you to pick the diagram type ie: candle, Bar, Line, Point, and Figure (seldom utilized as it is obsolete). You can likewise make a sweep or screener that is a bunch of directions for your stock picks. The PC accomplishes the work and you simply have a little rundown of stocks to browse. Recollect that your Broker isn't your companion. Each stock your intermediary prescribes is to make the representative affluent not you.

Altered settings for both Technical Indicators and Fundamental Indicators. You will change the settings for your exchanging style of the day.

Intraday exchanging, day exchanging, swing exchanging, and Momentum Trading are a couple of exchanging styles. Techniques are applied to a particular exchanging style FYI.

The capacity to keep up with notes, watchlists, and verifiable information inside the product so it makes easy to audit earlier exchanges rapidly.

Fantastic verifiable information on stocks, records, and so forth. Most representatives limit the verifiable information. This can be unfavorable to your productivity.

Choices Indicators assume that you exchange choices or any pointers pertinent to the monetary instrument you wish to exchange present moment.

Clean information that is dependable. Indeed, there is a quality distinction between graphs that you might use regarding the precision of the information.

Regardless of whether you utilize a Broker App on your Phone, you want solid, steady, dependable web access. Nothing is more irritating than to be in a profoundly productive exchange exit and afterward have the web waver or separate WiFi.

A Broker that offers a total arrangement of request types that are supported for retail exchanging. Numerous expert request types are not accessible to you yet regularly expedites offer fewer request type decisions that benefit them.

Great recordkeeping apparatuses. On the off chance that you have the IRS status of "Exchanging as a Business", these devices are basic. Be that as it may, you ought to have recordkeeping devices for exchanging regardless of whether you are ordered by the IRS as a "side interest broker". You might have to question a request fill or request exchange with your dealer eventually. This is intriguing yet it works out. Each specialist is expected to have a "Consistence Officer" that you can document a conventional protest with IF you accept that the request execution was outside the NBBO or other inappropriate fill. However, to record a grievance you should have documentation.

You likewise need what I call an "Exchange Management Planner" this is a straightforward program that gives you fundamental data about what value reach to exchange, the number of exchanges you need to do a month or seven days, the number of focuses you that need to give your part size, and significantly more. The Trade Management Planner is an instrument for dealing with your month-to-month payments so consistently you meet or surpass your pay objectives on a predictable month-over-month premise.

Risk Analysis Tools. You will require instruments to survey, examine, and control your risk. You ought to have Risk Analyzer Tools that dependably work out the chances of the exchange versus an expected benefit of each exchange. These are apparatuses that are normally essential for the stock pick investigation devices. Your full assistance diagramming project ought to likewise have cautions to control risk. What's more, your Trade Management Planner additionally is important for the risk the executives.

I'm certain this all sounds like a lot of devices and work. Yet, these devices are as of now made and intended for you so you should simply figure out how to utilize them.

Experts don't toss darts at the market and expectations for benefits. They use accuracy devices that increment their likelihood of accomplishment and never bet or surmise.

At the point when you utilize comparative exchanging devices, your pressure goes down, responsibility is decisively decreased, and benefits go up. Apparatuses for exchanging are significant.

Nonetheless, you needn't bother with a very costly exchanging stage. The vast majority of the apparatuses ought to be in your instructional class and others ought to have an ostensible month-to-month expense.

Keep in mind: to bring in cash, you should put resources into yourself and your schooling. There are no gifts in the monetary business sectors. Your specialist creates immense gains on each client they have whether or not that merchant brings in cash or misfortunes cash, the agent gets his cut.

Outlining and patten's of exchanging

A candlestick chart is the best diagram for anticipating the development of stock for day exchanging. 15 Min and 1Hr are the best periods to grasp the development of stock. The pattern is grasped in this diagram. Purchasers and dealers in each flame.

Combination in diagram help to foresee the stock future. Markers can undoubtedly place in this graph.

The candle is vital for day exchanging. It doesn't make any difference whether you are exchanging or effective money management however candle is vital on the off chance that you don't utilize a candle then it is exceptionally difficult to examine cost activity. There are many kinds of candlestick chart however one needs to grasp the total profundity of the candle

Each flame just like its own importance and if you use it appropriately, sooner or later we can anticipate the future cost activity movement. Using different candlestick chart we can make designs. With graph designs, it is not difficult to peruse the cost activity

Technical analysis

Specialized examination is a great innovation that can cause you to acquire benefits without realizing the subordinate's market.

You can simply do intra-day or swing exchanging through specialized examination. You want to comprehend the candlestick chart examples and procedures connected with it.

The understudies at ISM Institute of Stock Market are creating predictable gains in the market with the specialized examination. Join their total course or just specialized and advanced specialized for additional techniques.

Simply realize that specialized examiners couldn't care less about the organizations behind the stocks they exchange or their productivity.

Tragically, specialized examination (TA) isn't generally so basic as 'getting it done.' There are innumerable TA methods of reasoning, systems, and strategies - a significant number of which are legitimate and a considerable lot of which are presumably rubbish. Furthermore, tragically again it takes most dealers years to dominate the discipline. In any case, even at the ace level, you should be ready for things to conflict with you as you are continuously managing a component of irregularity.

Despite everything many individuals could say to you, TA is tied in with figuring out value, volume, and time (they are the main three factors that show up on a standard cost diagram). There's no need to focus on anticipating what's to come. Everything without question revolves around finding high-likelihood set-ups that have a higher possibility of working for you.

The thought is to utilize specialized examination to translate cost activity so you could exchange with the pattern or distinguish breakout designs.

How to pick a stock

Stock Pick choice requires a comprehension of what makes an incredible stock with outstanding cost development after some time if you have any desire to contribute long haul.

To exchange stocks for month-to-month payments, then it is a unique cycle. The accentuation for exchanging stocks isn't the organization because the hold length is a couple of days to a few weeks.

What is important in stock pick choice for exchanging stocks is to recognize the Professional

Trader's arrangements which permit you to enter the stock before the run-up starts. This requires Spatial Pattern Recognition Skills.

Additionally, a significant part of stock pick determination for all effective financial planning and exchanging styles is risk examination and hazard control.

Not all financial backers are large in stock picking. Numerous portfolios incorporate a couple of stocks that the financial backer thinks have potential (and that deliver profits). At the point when you choose to take a shot at stock picking, getting your work done is significant. You need a decent worth, particularly on the off chance that you intend to clutch something for some time. Here are a few things you ought to realize about an organization before putting away your well-deserved cash.

1. Check your feelings at the entryway
"Progress in financial planning doesn't connect with IQ … what you want is the disposition to control the urges that cause others problems in money management." this is alluding to financial backers who let their heads, not their guts, drive their effective financial planning choices. Truth be told, exchanging over movement set off by feelings is

quite possibly of the most well-known way financial backers hurt their portfolio returns.

2. Pick organizations, not ticker images

It's not difficult to fail to remember that behind the letters in order soup of stock statements slithering along the lower part of every CNBC broadcast is a genuine business. However, don't allow stock picking to turn into a abstract idea.Buying a portion or shares of an organization's stock makes you a section proprietor or shareholders of that business.

You'll encounter an astonishing measure of data as you screen potential colleagues. In any case, it's simpler to home in on the secret sauce while wearing a "business purchaser" cap. You need to know how this organization works, its position in the general business, its rivals, its drawn-out possibilities, and whether it brings a novel, new thing to the arrangement of organizations you currently own.

3. Does the organization have great basics?

To find the solution to this inquiry, there is a 2-minute drill to track down an essentially solid organization. Utilizing this drill, you can channel the sound organizations so you can continue to explore further. If the organization isn't serious areas of strength for essentially, is a compelling reason need to become familiar with its items/administrations, rivals, future possibilities, and so on.

4. Put forth Long-Term Goals-

For what reason would you say you are thinking about putting resources into the securities exchange? Will you want your money back in a half year, a year, five years, or longer? Could it be said that you are putting something aside for retirement, for future school costs, to buy a home, or to fabricate a domain to pass on to your recipients?

Before effective financial planning, you ought to know your motivation and the logical time, later on, you might need the assets. Assuming you are probably going to require your speculation returned inside a couple of years, think about another venture; the financial exchange with its instability gives no sureness that your capital will be all suitable when you want it.

By knowing how much capital you will require and the future moment when you will require it, you can compute the amount you ought to contribute and what sort of profit from your venture will be expected to deliver the ideal outcome. To assess how much capital you are probably going to require for retirement or future school costs, utilize one of the free monetary mini-computers accessible over the Internet.

5. Broaden Your Investments-
Experienced financial backers have played out all of the important examinations to recognize and measure their chance. They are likewise agreeable that they can distinguish any potential dangers that will imperil their situation, and will want to exchange their ventures before assuming a disastrous misfortune., "The most secure speculation technique is to tie up of your resources in one place and watch the bushel." That said, don't wrongly think you are extraordinary, particularly in your most memorable long periods of effective financial planning.
Value speculations generally have partaken in a return essentially above different sorts of ventures while likewise demonstrating simple liquidity, all-

out permeability, and dynamic guideline to guarantee a level battleground for all. Putting resources into the financial exchange is an extraordinary chance to fabricate huge resources and an incentive for the people who will be reliable savers, make the vital interest in significant investment to acquire insight, fittingly

How would I effectively pick a stocks?

Stock Pick determination requires a comprehension of what makes an extraordinary stock with dramatic cost development after some time to contribute long haul.

If you have any desire to exchange stocks for month-to-month payments, then it is a unique interaction. The accentuation for exchanging stocks isn't the organization because the hold length is a couple of days to a few weeks.

What is important in stock pick choice for exchanging stocks is to recognize the Professional Trader's arrangements which permit you to enter the stock before the run-up starts. This requires Spatial Pattern Recognition Skills.

Likewise, a significant part of stock pick determination for all financial planning and exchanging styles is risk investigation and change control.

Not all financial backers are enormous in stock picking. Numerous portfolios incorporate a couple of stocks that the financial backer thinks have potential (and that deliver profits).
 At the point when you choose to take a shot at stock picking, getting your work done is significant. You need a decent worth, particularly on the off chance that you intend to clutch something for some time. Here are a few things you ought to realize about an organization before putting away your well-deserved cash.

1. Abandon your feelings
what you want is the disposition to control the urges that cause others problems in effective money management.".
2. Pick organizations, not ticker images
It's not difficult to fail to remember that behind the letters in order soup of stock statements slithering along the lower part of every CNBC broadcast is a genuine business. Buying a portion of an

organization's stock or shares makes you a section proprietor of that business.

You'll go over a mind-boggling measure of data as you screen potential colleagues. Yet, it's more straightforward to home in on the secret sauce while wearing a "business purchaser" cap. You need to know how this organization works, its spot in the general business, its rivals, its drawn-out possibilities, and whether it brings a new thing to the arrangement of organizations you currently own.

3. Does the organization have great essentials?

To find the response to this inquiry, there is a 2-minute drill to track down a very basic level of solid organization. Utilizing this drill, you can channel the sound organizations so you can continue to research further. If the organization isn't on a very basic level solid, there is a compelling reason need to get more familiar with its items/administrations, rivals, future possibilities, and so on.

4. want to exchange their ventures before assuming a disastrous misfortune. "The most secure venture methodology is to tie up of your assets in one place and watch the bushel." That said, don't wrongly

think you are either great, particularly in your most memorable long periods of effective money management.

Value ventures generally have partaken in a return essentially above different kinds of speculations while likewise demonstrating simple liquidity, complete permeability, and dynamic guideline to guarantee a level battleground for all. Putting resources into the securities exchange is an extraordinary chance to construct enormous resources and an incentive for the people who will be predictable savers, make the vital interest in significant investment to acquire insight, fittingly deal with their chances, and are patient, permitting the sorcery of building to work

for them. The more youthful you start your money management diversion, the more noteworthy the eventual outcomes simply make sure to stroll before you start to run.

Individuals say that cash can't purchase satisfaction yet if you put it correctly and acquire more, certainly you will get some bliss. So I decided to put resources into financial exchange since it's a decent stage to put away cash.

Stock Exchange plan

exchanging plan is to safeguard you from your imperfections.

On the off chance that you don't have an arrangement and a reasonable grouping of activities, all that you truly do will be conflicting and irregular. Furthermore, irregular activities lead to arbitrary outcomes.

It doesn't have anything to do with a positive outcome or a ways off.

Market achievement is just repeatable and practical if there is a thoroughly examined process behind it.

For what reason do Forex Traders require an exchange plan?

How would I arrange to exchange?

What is your predictable intraday exchange plan?

An exchanging plan is what you compose when the market is shut that instructs you when the market is open.

Brokers who follow a restrained methodology are the ones who endure many years after years. Do you follow a restrained methodology? While exchanging as in many undertakings, it's essential to begin toward the end and work in reverse to make your arrangement and sort out what kind of broker you ought to be.

The best merchants exchange to design. Continuously record things on paper. Why? Since it will assist you with keeping fixed on your exchanging goals. An arrangement assists you with keeping discipline as a broker. It ought to assist you with exchanging reliably, dealing with your feelings, and even assistance to further develop your exchanging technique over the long run.

Continuously recollect that the exchanging plan is a work underway and the principal reason for exchanging plan is to keep you on task and to work compellingly and proficiently to go with great exchanging choices.

We figure out the stocks a day prior, mark the levels, and hang tight for the passage on the lookout

Pick Your Analytical Approach

The logical methodology responds to the inquiry, "how would you recognize exchange set-ups?". It very well may be a mix of value backing and opposition, pattern lines, graph designs, Fibonacci levels, moving midpoints, and so on.

This underlying step of the exchanging plan assists merchants with restricting their emphasis on a small bunch of situations that the dealer is OK with. From that point, dealers can search for chances to exchange given favored exchange setups. As of late, LiteFinance is giving a great giveaway challenge where you get an opportunity to win a pristine iPhone 13 Pro Max.

Select Your Favorite Trade Set Ups

The exchange setup is at the center of the exchange system. On the whole, consider the logical methodology and the occasion that sets off the exchange setup. An illustration of this would see a union example (recorded in the scientific methodology as a diagram design) which then, at that point, leads to ensuing activity from the broker, for example, the dealer will choose to exchange the breakout or sit tight for a pullback or consolidate breakouts with pullbacks solely after the diagram design has effectively worked out.

Limit the Markets to Focus on
While beginning, dealers genuinely must restrict the number of business sectors in the center. No market is something similar and restricting the extent of business sectors can help merchants to figure out the subtleties of the market being referred to. Brokers might zero in on unambiguous periods of a solitary market to comfort themselves with its qualities and developments.

Ponder Your Holding Period
Periods will rely upon the sort of dealer. Merchants that emphasize transient exchanges (exchanges opened and shut around the same time) incorporate hawkers and informal investors. Medium-term dealers ordinarily hold exchanges for a couple of

hours up to a couple of days and are alluded to as swing merchants. Long haul exchanging includes periods going from various days, weeks, months, and now and again, years.

Know Your Risk Tolerance
Each move toward the exchanging plan is significant, notwithstanding, assuming that risk the executives is feeling the loss, the entire arrangement will self-destruct. In this step, brokers should find their risk resistance which relates to how far a dealer will set stop misfortunes while restricting disadvantage risk.

Exchanging system or methodology

There is nobody's "best" Forex exchanging methodology. Various brokers will have various inclinations, contingent upon their risk resistance, exchanging style, and in general targets. Some normal Forex exchanging systems include: 1) Position exchanging: This procedure includes taking a drawn-out perspective available, and clutching exchanges for quite a long time or even a long time at a time. Position dealers normally center around significant money coordinates and exchange in light of basic examination. 2) Swing exchanging: This technique includes taking a more limited term perspective available and clutching exchanges for days or weeks all at once. Swing merchants commonly center around specialized investigation and search for valuable chances to enter and leave the market given cost designs. 3) Day exchanging: This methodology includes taking an exceptionally momentary perspective available and entering and leaving exchanges around the same time. Informal investors commonly center around specialized examination and search for chances to scalp little benefits out of the market. Which of these techniques is best for you will rely upon your very own conditions and targets.

what you want to make your mystery for the forex exchanging

acquire the greatest information on the forex market

learn everything about the specialized examination
comprehend the outline design
figure out how to draw the trendline
 learn cost activity

What is the best Forex exchanging methodology?

If anybody has any desire to be aware of the mystery of forex exchanging, then I should express that there could be regardless of which market you are exchanging like forex or stock wherever you want to become familiar with the market, you can not bring in cash without learning. On the off chance that you will learn better, you will acquire the best.

Before exchanging the forex market everybody ought to ascertain their chances and prize proportion, on the off chance that your risk and award proportion is positive, you can bring in cash in the forex exchanging. you don't require correctnesses like 80% or 90% if you are doing legitimate cash the executives, you can win the forex market with a half achievement proportion.

There is no pre-chosen mystery of the forex market you need to make your mystery for the forex market what you want to make your mystery for the forex exchanging

acquire the greatest information on the forex market

learn everything about the specialized examination

comprehend the graph design

figure out how to draw the trendline

The thing then you can make your mystery, another thing this everything will assist you with come by half outcome staying half outcomes rely upon your cash the executives on the off chance that you will exchange with great reward proportion, you can accomplish staying half too

I, first of all, need to say that I utilize symphonious examples in each examination and exchange I make, thus, the accompanying conversation is something that I solidly trust. Presently, what are consonant examples? They are a blend of basic and complex developments of specific proportions and their reciprocals through candlestick chart or bars that could demonstrate an inversion or in any event a remedy zone at specific levels. Likewise, with some other sort of examination, it is smarter to involve them related to others...

A lot of fledglings have asked me, "what is the best Forex exchanging system?" Everyone needs to know the solution to this inquiry, yet the fact of the matter is no technique is at any point ensured to work.

Anyway, there are a couple of things you ought to be aware of before you leave on your exchange venture. Since there are such countless various sorts of methodologies out

there, it's critical to recognize which ones fit you best.

There are two primary characterizations of money methodologies: major and specialized. Pattern exchanging falls into the subsequent arrangement. We should discuss what precisely pattern exchanging is and why it works!

Trend trading is effectively quite possibly the best system you can apply while exchanging the Forex market.

As the name recommends, this sort of technique includes exchanging the course of the ongoing cost pattern. To do so really, brokers should initially recognize the general pattern bearing, length, and solidarity to guarantee a reliably productive result.

There is no question that everyone is searching for the best forex exchanging technique. All things considered, it's a well-known fact that the Forex market is one of the most worthwhile on the planet. Also, there are many different exchange systems to learn.

And keeping in mind that the method I referenced above could work for different merchants, they probably won't be as viable for you.

So I prescribe you to give an initial shot of a demo account like the Olymp Trade demo record to check whether the procedure or method suits your exchanging style.

Risk management

Risk Management is the craftsmanship, science, cycle, and every one of the continuous exercises associated with recognizing, understanding, evaluating, checking, and afterward successfully lessening one's openness to risk, and the probability, effect, and unfortunate outcomes should any of those dangers emerge.

Even though dangers can be made due, it's essential to see the value in that dangers are continuously advancing (Old dangers can transform and change, while new, new dangers are continuously arising) and can never be disposed of.

Risk Measurement is the work to "evaluate" the probability and likely effect of a given risk or set of dangers happening. It's only one of the numerous potential components of chance evaluation.

Estimating risk is for the most part directed by utilizing likelihood and factual examination of memorable information that adjusts to a work of art "typical" ringer bend dissemination. Subsequently "standard deviation" is the most widely recognized unit currently utilized for risk estimation.

 the vital contrast between Risk and that's what uncertainty is that "Chance" can be estimated (utilizing factual strategies) and "Vulnerability" can't be estimated. That is so because the fluctuation of the scope of results of dubious peculiarities doesn't adjust to the chime bend dispersion model, and by definition can't be estimated.

Subsequently, it's critical to perceive the risk estimation is just solid when it's utilized in breaking down peculiarity where chime bend appropriation designs are the standard, (results are obscure, however, probabilities are referred to, for example, club betting, gambling machines, lottery, level, weight, and future.

Endeavoring to gauge risk in regions where vulnerability rules, (Outcomes are obscure and probabilities are obscure) like sentiment, war, seismic tremors, business, and contributing is defective and dangerous all along.

The domain of vulnerability is immensely bigger than the domain of hazard.

The individual who says that risk the executives must be completely powerful assuming it just is obliged by thoroughness drinks so many numb nuts mixed drinks each day, everything trust is lost. This individual doesn't have the foggiest idea of what they state or express. This doesn't have anything to do with coming over as a dick, an egotistical butt hole, haughtiness, no part of that is important. Assuming you work in chance, and that's what you hear, you clatter the right enclosure. The easiest analogy is seeing your child, who is plastered, move in the vehicle, and you hustle your butt around there. No kidding, "be cautious", you haul him out of the vehicle, all indecencies tossed at you by him to control you away, unessential, you did what you needed to. Save a daily existence.

Risk is only similar to a bath, which is spilling, and water streams to the place of least opposition. A speculation chief follows the path, recognizes its underlying driver, its utilization, reason, idea, and model, proposes a fix, future fixes, and continues.

Risk once got it, is where exchanging starts.

Many individuals have lost that capacity in today's world.

For risk, you don't need a degree, central comprehension of probabilities and math, basic reflection, and rational thinking abilities is a decent beginning stage. Its known as a library and a solid climate of friends who are mentally on a similar frequency share a similar speed or higher, never lower, a climate that pushes upwards or more, and could never make it, unremarkable and a safe place.

I've rarely seen a reality where inadequacy rules and everything that was required was Putin making perhaps of the most strategically most terrible conflict in history while almost everybody I realize broke quarter-breaking exchange returns, the best in their lives, even the veteran ones, while all nations meander around like headless chickens stressing over expansion and so forth. What leaves ivy schools and Oxbridge compatible with dreams in money should return to elementary school and begin once again when we simply center around the monetary space in this world.

Conclusion

Stocks can be an important piece of your speculation portfolio. Claiming stocks in various organizations can assist you with building your reserve funds, safeguard your cash from expansion and charges, and boost pay from your speculations. It's critical to realize that there are chances while putting resources into the securities exchange. Like any speculation, it assists with grasping the gamble/return relationship and your capacity to bear risk.

Advantages of putting resources into stocks.

Assemble. By and large, long-haul value returns have been exceptional than gets back from a cash or fixed-pay speculations like bonds. Notwithstanding, stock costs will quite often rise and fall over the long run. Financial backers might need to consider a drawn-out viewpoint for their value portfolio because these securities exchange variances will generally streamline over longer timeframes.

Safeguard. Assessments and expansion can influence your riches. Value ventures can give financial backers better expense treatment over the long haul, which can help slow or forestall the adverse consequences of the two assessments and expansion.

Amplify. A few organizations pay investors dividends1 or exceptional dispersions. These installments can furnish you with customary speculation pay and upgrade your return, while the positive assessment treatment for Canadian values can leave more cash in your pocket. (Note that profit installments from organizations beyond Canada are burdened unexpectedly.)

Various Stocks, Different Benefits

The two fundamental sorts of value ventures beneath can each offer financial backers various advantages.

1. Normal offers

Normal offers are the most (you got it!) normal sort of value venture for Canadian financial backers. They can offer:

Capital development.Many organizations deliver profits to their investors, which can be a wellspring of expense productive pay for financial backers.

Liquidity. Normally, normal offers can be traded more rapidly and effectively than different ventures, like land, workmanship, or gems. This implies financial backers can trade their venture for cash no sweat.

Favorable assessment treatment

2. Favored shares

Favored offers can offer financial backers the accompanying advantages:

Solid revenue source. Assortment,There are many sorts of favored shares, each with various highlights. For instance, some consider neglected profits to aggregate, while others can be changed over into normal offers.